S.H.I.N.E. INC.

THE GREATEST GIFTS OF ALL
Awareness, Self-Love, & Faith
By April Diane

S.H.I.N.E. Inc. Publications
Roosevelt, New York

DEDICATION

I Dedicate this Expression to my beloved Contrast
because of you challenging me I was able to rise during my
moment of truth.

To my beautiful family who always inspire me in only the way
family can
Mom, Dad, Tawana, Nkenge, & Nazyeir
I love you guys.

To my sacred sisters:
Two of my muses Kim Watts & Bolanile Richardson
your friendships are priceless!

To Moett AKA MoMo
If I could hand pick a daughter I'd pick you.

To my son:
Nazyeir Daiqwon thank you for all your wonderful ideas.
May you be filled with light and love always.

The Greatest Gifts of ALL

DISCLAIMER

The information contained in this book is not medical advice. Be sure to seek your doctor for any kind of treatment. Please note that the laws for naturopathic treatment vary from state to state.

No action should be taken based solely on the content of this book. Readers should consult appropriate health professionals on any matter relating to their health and well-being.

The information and opinions provided here are believed to be accurate and sound, based on the best information available to the author at this time. Readers who fail to consult appropriate health authorities assume the risk of any injuries. This book is not responsible for errors or omissions.

By reading this book, you assume all risks associated with using the advice contained within, with a full understanding that you, solely are responsible for anything that may occur as a result of putting the information into action in any way, regardless of your interpretation of the advice.

You further agree that the author cannot be held responsible in any way for the success or failure of your business as a result of the information presented below. It is your responsibility to conduct your own due diligence regarding the safe and successful operation of your business, if you intend to apply any of our information in any way to your business operations.

The Greatest Gifts of ALL

CONTRAST

WHAT YOU NO LONGER, AND PERHAPS NEVER DID,
DESIRE TO EXPERIENCE IN YOUR LIFE

OPPOSING TENSION

SHOWS UP AS:

ANGER, FRUSTRATION, FEAR, SADNESS ETC.

The Greatest Gifts of ALL

CONTRAST

Contrast leads the way to evolution
Creating desire for Divine Will
As I stand in the mist of opposition
I am propelled to be still
Blessing of patience revealed
Habit of prayer instilled
Practice of meditation installed
I am positioned to receive
As I bow in reverence humbly to
Higher vibrational frequencies
~ April Diane~

facebook.com/investinyouandshine
@investinyouandshine
@investnunshine
www.investinyouandshine.com

SCAN TO LISTEN

The Greatest Gifts of ALL

Forward

Life was like a movie being replayed over and over different characters same script. Like a hamster on a wheel I was going in circles only I would gain ground and get discouraged, give in to fears and regress back into the **samskaras** – habitual patterns I was so familiar with; until I wholeheartedly embraced the practices associated with yoga and meditation.

Through these practices, I learned that 'The Greatest Gifts of **ALL'** (The Divine) are the gifts of **awareness**, **self-love**, and learning how to practice **acts of faith** in the process.

The implementation of Yoga and Meditation was a paramount choice I made, changing the course of my life, allowing me to get off the hamster wheel, learn how to encourage myself, face the fears, and change my habits. The practice of yoga and meditation causes us to slow down, creating a pause in our lives. During that pause I was able to see, inner-stand, and embrace 'The Greatest Gifts of ALL.' These gifts are available to each one of us when we incorporate the practices of yoga and meditation into our lives.

The gifts: awareness, self-love, and faith, are concepts we can use to help us throughout the journey as we work to reach the goal of this experience which is to fulfill our individual purpose. The journey consists of four stages. These stages include: contrast, desire, alignment, and manifestation.

In this book I share with you how I learned to apply the greatest gifts of all, as I embraced the four stages throughout my journey to live life on purpose as a self-proclaimed, **Mind, Body, and Soul Wellness Guide**.

To sum it up, what I learned during my journey is that the contrast and the desire work together to help us align with the behavior and habits necessary to manifest our purpose. The challenge is that we first have to accept our true purpose. It is our perspective (how we feel about fulfilling our purpose), often referred to as our will, that is the deciding factor of when we fulfill our purpose. We ALWAYS get to CHOOSE how we will RESPOND. I was ready to choose a new way; create a new movie and change my script.

AWARENESS – CHAPTER 1

Let your awareness be your guide. ~ April Diane

It was time I got focused on what I wanted. Pure concentrated focus. The Divine kept sending me messages by way of beings in my life that I was giving way to much energy to the contrast. I was miss-understanding the purpose and intent of the contrast. You see, the Divine is always on purpose even when we are not aware.

As our awareness increases we begin to see that the contrast, things we do not want (opposing tension), are meant to be maps toward the things we do want. For a long time I was stuck judging the contrast. I felt I did not deserve to experience the pain it caused and because I refused to accept it, I could not see the lesson the pain caused and learn from the lesson. Until I became still and saw I was being prepared, I was being guided.

I started to let the contrast be my guide, triggers that propelled me to go deeper into my practices and the development of the necessary habits for raising my vibrational frequency enabling me to live life as my highest self. But before I tuned into the Gift of Awareness my contrast looked like this:

The Greatest Gifts of ALL

The Contrast

My mind was solely focused on what I and everyone did wrong, a victim of life expecting the worse and bracing myself for the pain. I spent my days judging things as good and bad with little time to live. I was feeling angry, jealous, depressed, afraid, lonely, broken, confused, and incomplete.

My Former Perspective:

As far as I was concerned, this experience had wronged me, served me up a healthy size of non-deserved pain, a pain I was born into and was not able to do anything about, a pain body of depression, self-doubt, insecurity, and dreams deferred.

The pain I felt wasn't my fault; it was handed to me, so why should I be responsible for the process of healing. Nobody else cared if I wrote, sung, fulfilled my dreams, so why should I? It's not that important. I'm not that important, besides there were other matters to be addressed. I had no time for fulfilling my dreams. I was too busy watching out for predators, the people and situations REALLY responsible for my inability to heal. I was on the case and I double dared anyone to get past me committing some unscrupulous act.

The Greatest Gifts of ALL

I was not taking responsibility for my actions or choices; in fact I did not even know how to make choices. Everyone else was to blame because I had given my power to external energy and as a result I felt everyone had and was committing a crime against me. With that said, I needed to keep the crime scene visible because one day there would be justice served and everyone who had done me wrong would pay.

I was taking names like the fictitious story of Santa Claus. I had a naughty and nice list. The only issue with my list was everyone eventually ended up on the naughty list. I made sure of it. I was creating the reality I believed to be true, based on the experiences I learned to identify myself with, based on the fact that I was secretly comfortable with the contrast.

The Truth:

Before I became aware, the contrast was my excuse and reason why I couldn't and wouldn't muster up the energy to do the work, however when I became aware it was also the very thing that helped me get to the truth.

Being a victim and keeping a list, was so much easier than it was to write a book, study for an exam, go to therapy, develop a plan, work through the plan, stick to the plan, you get the point. Keeping a list exhausted my time and took up my energy, so that I could fill my days and escape from doing my work. I was afraid.

Afraid of the risk! Lurking in the back of our minds there is always the possibility that we may not get what we work toward. I was afraid that I would try and still end up in the same place I started, in fact I had actually experienced this reality enough to believe this to be the end all be all reality. Additionally, there was that idea that when I got better it meant that someone got away with the abuse inflicted upon me.

On some level the pain was my friend, it was the one thing I could count on for sure. It was the one constant in my life. I was trying to honor the pain by holding on to the scars making sure they were visible, because if they disappeared I would have no proof and no reason to stay stuck – no excuses. I would have to do that work.

I would have to learn how to listen, honor, and follow my heart. I would have to learn to say no and not care if this meant I would lose 'friends.' I would have to be okay with going alone if I did not have someone to accompany me on my journey, and ultimately I would have to let go of the story, the one thing I thought I knew for sure.

The Greatest Gifts of ALL

The Story:

As a child, some of the experiences I went through gave me the impression that I was unworthy and of no value, and needed to just deal with things even though they made me feel bad.

Indeed I had experienced some sinful moments, moments without representation of love present; the challenge was I built my identity around those moments. For a long time when I would connect with people I would lead with my victim story. It went something like this, "Yes I know I could do better, I know I'm talented, beautiful, deserve more, buuuuttttt, I am a victim of molestation so don't expect too much from me. (Well I did not necessarily always verbalize this, however; the energy I used at the time expressed this sentiment).

I was stuck in the story. I suppose I believed if I got to the root of the why, I could either undo it, feel better, get someone to admit they were wrong, or all of the above would work too.

Additionally, I was seeking justification for the victimization I'd placed on myself. There is nothing worse than self-abuse. It grips a hold of you and then it's hard to turn it loose because once you become aware you don't want to believe what YOU have now also done to YOU.

Before the total awareness point I had glimpsed the revelation of what I was sent here to do, I knew who I was called to be I just didn't know how to execute it, and by golly I couldn't find the time between my 24 hour list making endeavor, I WAS TOO BUSY BEING A VICTIM TO SUCCEED!

At around 33 I started the process of being **aware** of this condition of my mind that was helping to continue certain patterns in my life. I became aware that because I was identifying myself as being a victim, I was unconsciously making myself a victim in every situation to fit the character I was playing. I learned to accept this awareness long enough to learn how to make some effective changes.

I didn't want to be a victim any longer. Slowly I learned by practicing yoga & meditation that I could choose another way and change my life. It was the longest ahhhahh moment I had ever experienced. I COULD CHOOSE!

You see in the mind of someone identifying with the victimization they've experienced there are no choices. You 'I' had to listen to and continue to debate with the voices of the critiques in my head scrutinizing my every move. I had to continue engaging in unhealthy relationships because if I didn't this would dismiss my list taking role and clear up the crime scene I was working so hard to preserve. Men were jerks, disgusting, one track minded, selfish, pedophiles who couldn't be trusted. End of story.

There was no choice this case had to be proven. Maybe somewhere in my mind I thought if I would prove the case to the Divine strong enough the naughty list makers would be annihilated from existence and the world would finally have some peace. Yeah, about that.

Choosing takes work, practice, patience, and time. What I didn't realize was I WAS choosing. I was choosing to be a victim, choosing to listen to the critiques instead of learning ways to drown them out. Choosing men with certain behavior patterns because quite simply put, they were easy. Easy not to get caught up in, because I wasn't really that in to them so there was no real risk if things did not work out.

Choosing to fill my days with drama and other people's life lessons because I was ultimately afraid: afraid that maybe I really wasn't anything but a typical statistic of a race, community, and culture filled with self-hate lacking the ability to accomplish anything meaningful, inflicted with a generational curse that no matter how hard we tried to shake it we couldn't, doomed from before conception.

The beautiful thing about **awareness** is at first it smacks you with what is: seeds blossomed planted with unconscious actions. And then it leads the way to what could be. The two go hand and hand you literally cannot have one without the other. So many times when awareness revealed some phenomenon about myself to me, I had to shake away the urge to feel guilty and beat myself up about past seeds planted yielding an unwanted crop.

I couldn't get hung up on the weeds because ultimately once my awareness was intact I could see their purpose. I could see how they helped shape and define the garden I really wanted to plant. You know, learning from my mistakes. They were my best teachers painting a very clear picture of the type of garden I didn't want, showing me very plainly what not to do. They became my learning curve like the cones aligning the scene of an accident on the highway screaming 'stay the speed limit, keep your eyes on the road, no texting or you could end up like this.'

Additionally, I couldn't get hung up on the weeds because that would take me back down the road of being a victim and I was on the path leading toward being a victor. I could

The Greatest Gifts of ALL

hear the victim story sequel now "Oh look at what I've done to myself, I can't write a book now I waited too long, I can't marry again I already screwed up two marriages." Yeah, been there done that, not going there. It was time to close that chapter, finish the book, and CHOOSE not to be a victim.

Many times throughout the process I felt like I was lost at sea, I felt like giving up. I learned instead how to take a break when the process of transforming became overwhelming. While change is inevitable it's not always, almost never, well received because it requires work, effort, time, patience, and practice. Energy usually used on something else. These habits, patience and practice, alone must be cultivated and once they are one can accomplish anything.

Changing and transforming, focusing our energy on living as our higher-self and not a victim is just the endeavor equipped to handle the cultivation of patience and practice I would need to learn how to close the chapter, finish the story and work on creating a new one on purpose. This understanding took time. I had a lot of stuff stored up inside of me, heck my naughty list alone was almost the size of Webster's dictionary with a new edition published yearly!

The Greatest Gifts of ALL

I had experienced a lot of moments without taking the time to acknowledge and identify my feelings and the role I played in these experiences, causing me to experience them over and over again. This eradication of identifying with the victim mentality was going to take time. I had to build my muscle for it, almost similar to going to the gym. I had to break through walls of resistance. Identifying these walls as the most important muscle building moments, the hard stuff.

During the Awareness Point the Walls Started Coming Down I Began to...

1. Relinquish the urge to tell the victim story

2. Release the urge to lie in bed when a bike ride would make me feel better

3. Release the urge to gain external approval and validation

Over time I developed the habit surrounding this idea, life is a series of simulations meant to help you fulfill your purpose, and your soul is drawing to you what you need to evolve. Each experience you have, whether you deem it good or bad in your mind is an opportunity to grow. The deciding factor is your perspective and when you understand that you can choose not to experience it again by the way you respond.

I began to ask the Divine what is the message in this part of the story. What am I supposed to gain out of this? So I found myself in the mist of painful experiences practicing stillness and asking the Universe what's the lesson here this victims gotta go!

Suggested Take Away

1. Learn to accept the contrast long enough to make some effective changes.

2. Use the contrast to fuel you toward creating something new, every time it shows up get still, go within, take steps to see how you are helping to create what you are experiencing.

3. Take time to process and acknowledge your feelings, use them as directional guides toward your higher self.

4. Ask what the message is so you can learn the lesson.

Awareness…

"And the day came when the risk to remain in a bud, was more painful than the risk it took to blossom" ~Anais Nin

Over 30 years it took me to close my heart, build up walls to protect myself from being hurt and yet I was still filled with so much pain, my heart was black and blue and my mind was attempting to destroy whatever bit of life that wanted to come my way.

Yes, over 30 years of living like this and now I realized the walls had to come down. The lock on my heart had to be removed for the pain of keeping these walls up was eating away at my soul. I had to find a way. It's really weird how we are taught, well at least I was taught in my culture, to die a little every day. Well that is what happens when you repress your feelings. It's very subtle too, so you have to be paying attention.

Looking at pictures of me growing up was extremely helpful in the process of connecting back to my heart. It was almost like I would go back in time for a moment because I can remember exactly how I was feeling in every picture. The pictures all pretty much say the same thing for me. Who are you? When are you going to allow yourself to really and truly express how you feel in a way that honors you, instead of having temper tantrums and holding silent vigilant sessions with yourself?

When, April Diane, are you going to allow yourself to honor God and live from your heart? During points over the years the images were taken, if I had to answer that question the answer would have been never. I was so afraid of being mocked, teased, ridiculed for expressing or "being in my feelings", or ultimately feeling neglected or avoided because people were afraid that I would want to TALK about how I felt.

Please understand that I would jump into my heart over the years, however; I was so not used to speaking through her that when I spoke from my heart I shouted, cried, or went way too hard to prove a point. Which ended up making me feel so lonely, at first, so I was afraid of going the distance? I would get right to the part when I let her open up, then any little denial of my feelings would shut the door back, because the idea of loneliness crept up.

I didn't realize that loneliness was just the first side effect of living from the heart. It's the experimental part. The part where you are in full observation mode, you know, taking inventory to see what's in there.

The Greatest Gifts of ALL

Now that I've stayed the course longer I see it got greater later, I realize some of that stuff/people I was trying hold on to needed to be renovated any way. Not in a negative way, but just like the puzzle pieces just didn't fit what my heart needed anymore. When we try to stay in situations that no longer serve us we are ultimately holding ourselves back from growing.

When we stay the course and learn to accept the contrast for what it is we become aware of how it is being created. The little "f" word FEAR that caused us not to want to look beyond to what we could not see miraculously gets transformed to the Big "F" word FAITH and little by little we learn there is life after the story fades, that we can heal from the pain.

We learn that little by little we can learn to live with and on purpose by healing the pain instead of tripping on the pain every time it shows up. Ultimately we learn that there really is such a thing as purpose and that everything we experienced was and is a part of that purpose, pain & all. I always marvel at how something's opposite causes you to seek "it" out. Isn't' life beautiful! The annoyance of the contrast sheds light on desire and the desire fuels us by encouraging us to become aware of the possibility of what we were not before able or willing to explore.

The Greatest Gifts of ALL

Despite the odds, when we are sick we search for a cure. In the process of finding the cure we also find peace. This works the same across the board. When we are lost we seek directions discovering new territory along the way, making new friends and learning more about ourselves.

When we fall down we look for ways to find strength and while pulling ourselves up we build muscle we never even knew existed. When we are without funds we learn how many resources are available to us and ultimately we learn that we don't need as much as we thought we did to feel happy.

One of the hardest truths I faced on this spiritual journey was the simple fact that there is nothing outside of me that will sooth my soul. Not a car, not a cat, not a man, not a hat, not trip to a faraway land. The way to sooth the soul is to listen to ALL it beholds. To inner-stand that the soul has purpose when it arrives to this grand experience we call life.

All the experiences we encounter are directly related to help us connect with that soul purpose. We can choose to judge the experiences as good or bad directing our emotions toward feeling happy or sad, which is fine as long as the judging directs our energy toward how to make more effective choices and when it's out of our control if the

The Greatest Gifts of ALL

judging of the emotions does not keep us stuck inside a spiral that stunts our growth. We can also learn to process them as purposeful tools each moment asking the Divine how this experience will help me to grow.

While I can share, dissect, and contemplate the conditions the soul finds itself in with friends, family, strangers, therapist etc. at the end of the day, in the still of the night, I must decide what these conditional feelings will make of me. I must decide how to use them and to determine this I must go to the source the ALL of what created me to be; enabling me to see how much bigger this experience can be for me. So the question became:

Would I identify with every moment attaching myself to each resisting the only thing constant in the world, change? Or would I allow the moments to pass through me like lessons from the Master adding character teaching me how to give praise and rise above the things that challenge me, which would ultimately allow me to develop a new way of being, and allow me to continue moving forward toward my souls purpose focused and on assignment, bringing something extraordinary to this experience.

That is where I am, at the end of this chapter. A place of acceptance so bitter sweet I dare not eat till the end.

The Greatest Gifts of ALL

Instead I will savor the moments as they come, take responsibility for the choices I make; give myself permission and time to grow, learn to set boundaries as necessary, and ultimately listen to my heart and following my dreams, not allowing anything to distract me from fulfilling my soul's purpose.

God had a place for me at the head of the table, and because of the pain, anger, guilt, shame, and most of all fear I was holding on to, I had allowed myself to continue to eat the scraps dropped on the floor. Doors would close, one of the ways God used to redirect me, and I would run full speed ahead pushing them back open. Demanding to be heard and demanding to be respected.

As I begin to understand and respect the process of living a life of purpose, I understood better that it was not necessary for me to demand anything. It was not necessary for me to beg to be heard. Everything I needed and deserved God had waiting for me. All the while God was positioning me to receive all I deserved every time a door was closed. Not necessarily because what was behind the door was 'bad', it just wasn't what I needed or what I was ready for at that time.

The Greatest Gifts of ALL

So I did not need to keep a list of people crucifying them for their actions and behaviors. I only needed to learn to love myself enough to listen to my heart, and honor how I felt, and make sure I was not actively participating in activities that did not serve me, and take responsibility for me. Understanding that every moment was a lesson, and everyone I encountered was a teacher. It's a beautiful experience I felt to finally understand that God had my back all the time. It was me and my perspective not understanding the simplicity of the lesson.

I was not in charge of controlling external factors. I simply was in charge of connecting with me, you know, 'seek ye first the kingdom/queendom of heaven' and everything would unfold according to Divine design. What to do next, what direction to take this guidance was placed right in the center of my being, right in my heart. I just simply had to listen and open up to my feelings.

I learned what the contrast looked like, sounded like, acted and felt like. This awareness directed me like those warning signs on the parkway to say a prayer, take a deep breath, spend some time in meditation, and practice some yoga.

As a result, new habits were forming; habits of trusting the process, habits of walking by faith and not by sight. I started inner-standing that seeds were germinating in the dirt even though I could not see the flower yet. I simply had to keep watering the seeds and allowing them to get enough sunlight.

I grew

In love with laughter
Forgiveness
Self-love
Compassion
Focus &
Commitment

I became

Determined to decide my destiny
to set my soul free
allowing myself to be who I am created to be

My purpose

To inspire myself & others to live from within

I walked

In faith and not by sight

The Divine

Helped me find the light

Through the struggle, the pain, & the uncertainty

I learned

To dance in the rain

Enabling me to find:

'The Greatest Gifts of ALL'

The Greatest Gifts of ALL

Desire

THE DREAMS IN YOUR SOUL YOU'RE BORN TO
EXPERIENCE

"I AM THAT, IAM"

~ The Divine

So now that I was aware that it was up to me and that I could choose how I responded to life and each moment was directing me to my souls purpose, no matter good or bad, and now that I had made a definitive decision that I no longer wanted to be a victim, that I was going to do the work, dig deep and take whatever steps were necessary, that I wasn't going to let conditional feelings define me, I was ready for the next step.

I have confidence and courage to be inner directed, this was my centering thought on the day I attracted into my experience a yoga class that aligned with my thinking. Just like that preparation meets opportunity.

'YOU ARE THE BOSS' I heard the yoga instructor say and it sounded like music to my ears. You are the boss. I had to catch myself. I almost started looking around; my mind secretly wondered who she was talking about.

Did she mean me? And if she did who was she saying I was the boss of? Did she mean me? No she couldn't mean me. I had to chuckle, of course she did.

The Greatest Gifts of ALL

Those simple words 'YOU ARE THE BOSS' fueled me up like a shot of vitamin B12. I felt empowered, on top of the world. "I'm running this," my heart shouted. Then the contrast kicked in; in the form of doubt & fear. At that very moment, I affirmed; I am that, I am and reminded myself that the Divine did not give us the spirit of fear. I Took a deep breath and listened to the lesson as the Divine was revealing it to me in real time.

The Lesson:

We come to this experience to learn the truth. To see who we really are. To learn how to see ourselves the way God sees us, pure & whole. This experience, based on what the Divine has shared with me on my journey, is simply a series of simulations meant for us to connect back with that truth; a purification process. The old me, well the uninformed, disconnected part of my story looked at life in a disconnected way. However, everything is connected.

Why is that important to mention here you ask? Great question, I used to see other beings (people, animals, etc.) as something outside of myself. However, now I know we are all a part of each other mirroring ourselves to one another for the purpose of self-reflection and growth. I know that is a pretty out of the box idea and it may seem pretty

The Greatest Gifts of ALL

farfetched, considering how we've been taught to relate to one another. However, I've glimpsed it, and it's true. I am you.

So when the yoga instructor (a part of me) reminded me that I was the boss. She simply was sharing with me that I was in charge of what I was experiencing. I was co-creating the simulations I went through based on my soul's needs and reediness. Nothing in essence was happening outside of me. It was all taking place inside me. And as I connected with myself more, listened to my heart, the reflection was becoming clearer. I could see the truth.

I could see what I believed about myself (without the Divine's perspective). I could see how that belief was influencing my thoughts, actions, and ultimately my every day experiences. This was huge. No one was victimizing me, my disconnection from the Divine was causing me to be off balance, with a blurry vision of who I was and so I was attracting the same type of experiences to me from the time of birth. Yes we are always choosing. Choice is a major part of the simulation exercises. The question we are sent here to answer is will we choose the Divine. We've always been on this purposeful mission way before we connected with human concepts and time.

The Greatest Gifts of ALL

Suggested Take Away

- Create a list of Divine inspired affirmations
- Anytime you are challenged by the contrast showing up as fear and doubt, repeat these affirmations to remind yourself who you really are.

ALIGNMENT

GETTING YOURSELF INTO POSITION:
REPROGRAMMING YOUR THOUGHTS AND CHANGING YOUR
ACTIONS

Rising to Victory

As I stand in my moment of truth
Will I fall or will I rise
Sensations of fear
Pulsate through my being
I breath deeply
Seeking guidance from the laws
Create in me a new way
A true way
A habit of evolutionary proportion
Removing distortion
Rejuvenate my essence which is Divine
Transport me to a time and place mentally
Where this is all resolved
Finding me sitting on my throne
All is well
In faith I stand
Knowing truth is all that is real
Transforming what I feel into
What I desire to be
Concentrating my energy
Rising to VICTORY

~ April Diane ~

SCAN TO LISTEN

facebook.com/investinyouandshine
@investinyouandshine
@investnunshine

www.investinyouandshine.com

The Greatest Gifts of ALL

Awareness…

When you make a decision to change, your old habits will behave like little children who want to have their way. Kicking and screaming trying to make you give in to them. **IT IS A TEST**. MOMENTS OF TRUTH.

During the alignment process, they were all coming up. Every fear I ever had, fear of lack was the biggest one, lack of love, lack of money, lack of time, lack of trust, lack of respect, and lack of faith. Because of my new awareness, you know about this experience being one big lesson and all, I was in a position to heal all those thoughts and beliefs of lack. I knew they stemmed from me being disconnected from the source. When they came up this time, I had to CHOOSE a new way to respond so that I would create a new habit, a habit that would align me the Divine.

Every painful experience was ultimately a chemical, neurological reaction to that disconnection. I was being trained by the Universe to be a healing guide, on the job training. As my pen meets this paper and I share with you my heart and lessons, I am taking the time to focus on what I want to attract in my life. I want to attract healing in these areas of believing in lack. The samskaras (impressions, memories) so deeply rooted in my nervous system. I feel the sensations and by now for sure I've done enough work to know where they stem from. So how could they be healed? I had to learn to release them, and choose a new way when they showed up.

Now instead of acting in accordance with the pain making it deeper by burying the feeling or energizing it more by venting about it AGAIN I would CHOOSE to cleanse my chakras (energy channels) by taking a deep breath. A choice I am making to energize the healing, breathing in wellness, exhaling everything that no longer serves me.

Now my Moments of Truth, the moments I am challenged by the most because the scars are showing up, caused me to evolve, transform and grow. They caused me to align with a new way of being. When I felt pain, I got out my pen and began to write. When I felt anxious I would talk myself into a bike ride or my new favorite, a yoga session.

The seeds I sowed before were presenting themselves as they had always showed up in my life, however; I was different now, I was aware, how awesome is that! I could see them, I had learned to pause long enough to identify them and that was the Gift. I'm reminded of what my dad told me so many years ago, **"To be aware is to be alive."** (I know he probably thought I wasn't listening, however; I was

The Greatest Gifts of ALL

I just did not know at the time what that meant). Now that I did, I realized that the knowledge of this awareness gift meant one thing only, I WAS COMING ALIVE BABY, and it felt AMAZING!!!!

I was going to use this powerful moment of truth where my mind is at its peak point of awareness of this circumstance to uproot those seeds and dig them out all while simultaneously planting new seeds. ALIGNMENT!!!!! My new best friend.

My Lesson:

I had come to understand I wasn't being punished I was being blessed. Even though at times I felt alone, I was alone with peace. The things that were no longer serving had not only been removed, they had been replaced. The Divine was helping me learn how to invite peace into my life. A practice that like everything else took time to master and time was ALL I had. I learned to welcome the journey and to enjoy the lessons and to use the lessons to ALIGN.

I began to see that life was all God. The pain, the bliss, the sun and the rain it all led me back to the exact same place communicating with the Divine. I remember a monumental moment I had with the Divine. I said you know God if I had a dollar for every frustration, anguish, pain, perceived failure, etc. I would be RICH! The response from the Divine was, "well you are already RICH by my standard, so now go use that STUFF you call frustration, anguish, pain, and perceived failure to make you financially wealthy!"

You see what I mean by it's all God! Even when the pain was rejected, ignored, or overlooked on some level I was still communicating with the Divine. Whether the pain expressed showed up as feelings of anger or singing God's praises we were talking, connecting and eventually I learned to realize these opportunities, **MOMENTS OF TRUTH** were an important part of the development and alignment of higher self. A time out, a pause the teacher had to get my attention and causing moments of truth was the most effective way, for me any way, to cause me to seek light. We became one during these moments. Me seeking the Divine, the Divine seeking me.

Aligning with the lesson:

So once I got the lesson it was on and popping! I had a moment, well heck MANY challenging moments in one day, I started calling them a Day of Truth!

On a cold winter day in 2014, what I deemed the COLDEST WINTER EVER SEQUAL, I seemed to be experiencing nothing but contrast after contrast. You name it, my weeds were coming to the surface, my awareness to the weeds was in full view and I had no one (it seemed) to turn to but me. So I said, okay April Diane, what in the world is your beautiful creative self-going to do? Because I was equipped with the knowledge of my newest lesson (ALIGNMENT) it was time to turn that knowledge to wisdom and apply the theory, make it a practice. I was hungry, literally and figuratively, yeah the fridge was looking a little scarce. Bills were turning into Williams, and I could do one of two things, I could fall or I could rise. It was time to RISE! I sought out an opportunity. I got in my car, took out one of the many fliers and proposals I had created for my business and I drove to one of the local libraries to pitch my proposal. I had to energize my desire; I had to find a way to bring light into this dark **moment of truth** I was experiencing.

I walked into Freeport library, crochet connection proposal in hand, dressed in one of the only suits I owned at the time, with a desire and a prayer. My actions were the exact action I needed to align myself with the manifestation of my desire. I had to push and encourage myself to grow in the direction of my dreams. It was not easy; my mind was replaying everything I was seeing at the time. I had to shake it off; I could not honor those feelings by adding to them. I had to figure out a way that I could free myself from that

The Greatest Gifts of ALL

experience in the future. I had to choose, in the mist of the moment, another way.

The alignment process often feels like an internal battle. You seem to be so aware of everything you do not want at the moment. It's almost like your mind is pulling up your moment of truth file! Every bill you owe, every perceived failure, every unpleasant experience, and every reason not to rise surfaces, along with the vision of what it would feel like to be on the other side of this challenging moment in victory.

Then silently comes that thought, "do I really have what it takes?" Well I am here to tell that if you keep practicing you build the courage and the stamina to have what it takes, so while you may not feel like you have what it takes right then in that moment, if you keep practicing you better believe you will and the only way you will truly know and believe, is if you go the distance.

I went the distance, not knowing what to expect, facing the fear of being rejected, the fear of failure. I walked into that library during my moment of truth. I spoke to the library programmer, and to my surprise they had a program already in place like the one I was proposing. I proceeded to leave, still submitting my proposal, because you never know, life

The Greatest Gifts of ALL

changes all the time that is actually one of the things we can count on for sure (evolution). As I was leaving I had one of those famous ah ha moments I had been prone to, ever since my mind started thinking in the way of solution development. I took a look at the libraries latest newsletter and noticed they didn't have another program I could offer, Yoga.

Taking my yoga certification was another phenomenal alignment activity the Divine opened up for me, that I embraced (KEY WORDS – 'I EMBRACED'). So I walked back toward the programmer's office and I said, "Do you have a yoga class in place, I did not notice one in the newsletter." Like music to my ears she said, "You are right on time! I am so glad you came back!" "When do you have a space open?" Not only did we schedule a series of yoga classes at the Freeport library, she connected with me with an annual library event that allowed me to connect with over 50 librarians in one day. This event propelled S.H.I.N.E. Inc. to experience the necessary growth and development to sustain itself during the 2nd year of its doors opening up and beyond. I had successfully, used the alignment process to RISE during my Moment of Truth.

The Greatest Gifts of ALL

Suggested Take Away

- Keep your eyes on the prize
- When the contrast shows up, know this is a disconnected chemical reaction in your body that occurs when you are out of alignment with the Divine
- Get connected (Pray & Meditate) then move forward toward your goal.
- Focus on the solution

Dear Higher Self

Dear Higher Self
As I Gravitate toward you
I hear you calling for me
I feel you wanting me
to simply ALLOW you to be
Release me from fear set my wings
FREE so I may fly high above
The doubts that try
to suffocate my dreams
for I belong with you
As I relinquish
The temptation to resist
The lighter I feel
In the mist of the
Raging of the storm
I shall not conform
to the madness
trapped inside the belly of the beast
I shall execute my souls purpose
Triumphantly
The momentum builds
as I climb higher
Breath she beckons me
From beneath the layers of the seen
Dream April Dream
She softly whispers in between
The ideas racing through
The dramatic scenes
As they brew the soup
that appears to be my life
Creatively I decline
Turning ashes into masses
Of healing
moments of doubt trigger the reminder
To go higher
Practice the FEELING
Ignite the healing of my soul
I behold thee in me
So I've come to collect what is mine
during a time when hell is breaking loose
giving way to heaven
the lucky number seven
completes me simplistically
Dear Higher Self
Consume me
Groom me like
A new born
Reborn
Un-torn
I remember you
We've met in the crevices of my mind
When I was blind
to social standards
Cliquish banter
Judgmental faces
Replacing
Loving embraces
You are my essence
You give me life
Unconditionally
As no condition
Dictates you love for me
Dear Higher Self
~ *April Diane*

The Greatest Gifts of ALL

Self –Love – Chapter 2

The Story:

After reading a few pages of Deepak Chopra's 'A Path to Love' I realized I was expecting love to come from some external source.

The Lesson:

The internal guided voice within me reminded me that I could only experience what I already had within. A revelation that empowered me to seek out what it meant to love me.

Unconsciously I was thinking 'I will love you April when someone else shows they love you.' I was searching for that missing piece that would make me lovable confused about what love really meant, and where it came from. For years my unconscious definite chief aim when I arose in the dawn was to be as lovable as possible.

I tried too hard, gave too much, and found myself exhausted stressed, irritable, angry, desperate, needy, mean, with the entity in which I sought love from looking at me like what is wrong with you. I can laugh about it now, because I evolved, which is a great feeling.

The Greatest Gifts of ALL

Secretly nobody wants to be around desperation, most people shy away from neediness, and if you are not able to show yourself love people see that and run because they don't want to experience what you are feeling. You may receive at the very least toleration, some pity, you may be used, and if you're not careful you may experience abuse.

I realized I had neglected self-love. The love of self, because I didn't know it was okay to give love to myself. I really thought it came from outside of me. It was a topic that kept coming up for me, so like everything else I seek to understand I had to do some research.

Lately since I've developed the habit of beginning within I start my research with meditation, yoga, a bike ride to what has now become one my favorite places 'Roosevelt Park,' and an expression of my thoughts were my pen meets the pages of my journal.

This research process led me to the question, "how do you show love?" The answers came in abundance and they were as follows: being kind, patient, gentle, truthful, helpful, nurturing, and supportive. So right then I realized that I needed to conduct an assessment of the activities I carried out each day to see if those activities fit into my definition of love I devised.

The Greatest Gifts of ALL

One of the things I understood was the law of attraction and that I was attracting to me that which I already was. So another part of the assessment included me taking inventory of my current experiences, the people I encountered on a daily basis and what these components said about my current vibration level.

The most important point I should mention about conducting an assessment is to understand there is no good or bad here. I was merely conducting the assessment to see how close I was to obtaining my definite chief aim, which is now to heal myself, and to develop a strategy for raising my vibration level to the optimum level required to reach my goal of self-love which is so important for the healing process.

A thought came to mind that is important to mention. I had to understand that I did not need any one to agree with me that I was worthy of this self-love. I had exclusive rights to the amount of love I wanted to show myself.

I did not need permission to be more loving and I did not need the approval of anyone or thing. For some reason this thought alone rendered me more enthusiastic about this process I was undertaking. I was the judge and the jury, the

Alpha and the Omega. You know, 'She da Boss!' It was that moment that I decided I would love myself to life.

My Message:

I am, that I am, a shining being dwelling in light manifested by the limbs of the ALMIGHTY DIVINE Creator, and I have a right to feel love, I have a right to abundance, I have a right to live in faith, and I choose to honor myself and these rights by taking the time to do the work required to align myself with these rights.

I am important and my feelings deserve to be felt honored and listened to, so I will honor and listen to my feelings. Not because I have to, but because I want to. Not because it's my fault that I feel this way, however; because it's my responsibility to love, honor, respect, and protect this experience I represent known as April Diane.

She is counting on me to give her time. She is counting on me to listen to her heart; she is counting on me to position myself in such a way that her dreams would come true. She and her feelings were my first priority. As I honor her with this new understanding, then and only then can I fulfill wholeheartedly the work I've been called to do.

The Greatest Gifts of ALL

As I showered myself with the things I sought to come from out there I realized how much I had in me. I realized I had ALL I needed to feel whole and complete and I realized the Divine was setting me up to be much more of a blessing to those I encountered because I was becoming the message.

I represented healing, I represented love, and I now represented what it meant to be in the flow of abundance. There is no greater inner standing of an idea or a concept than one's ability to see the result of the work.

Before people (we) have faith, we want to see, however; before we can truly see we have to trust and before we can trust we must believe that we are worthy. The steps I started taking to align myself showed I was beginning to believe, trust, and have faith in me. I and every experience I had was the message.

The Greatest Gifts of ALL

Self-Loving Assessment

Current self-loving behavior:
1. Study myself and my behavior
2. Care for my body by eating good nutritious
3. Educate myself daily
4. Express my feelings in a journal
5. Spend time being creative with my talents
6. Spend time with my family

Non-Self-Loving Habits to release:
1. Being overly critical of myself
2. Rushing myself to complete projects
3. Over committing myself
4. Not listening to how I feel by honoring those feelings with boundaries and better choices
5. Not highlighting my talents enough in my life
6. Engaging in romantic relationships that do not serve my purpose or highest self
7. Being aggressive & impatient with myself and my son during our learning process

Self – Loving Assessment Continued…

What I was attracting to me:
1. People being aggressive with me
2. Lack of effective management in my business affairs
3. Lack of support in the things that were important to me
4. People who were not truly interested in me as a person, but more so interested in what I could assist them with sexually, financially, emotionally etc.
5. Lack of success in my commitments

Self-Loving Habits I would like to incorporate more into my life style:
1. Spending more time working on my passions (writing & crocheting)
2. Pampering myself more often
3. Speaking kindly to myself

4. Choosing and engaging in balanced relationships that honor my desire to be loved, supported, and respected

I included in the assessment activities that I engaged in over the span of my life so that I could see how I've already grown in my quest for self-love and also as a reminder during moments I don't feel like being loving of what I could experience again, as inspiration to stay the course.

Expecting love to come first from an external source is something that challenges many beings. This is a dis-ease in and of itself. It is in fact the worst disease one can encounter and one of the most challenging ones to cure.

Fear is often the cause of many of the symptoms exhibited and surfacing in any disease. Fear of losing love brings on the loose of love, because it causes us to become and exhibit anxious and worried behavior that can make us attempt to control the natural flow of life by the way of force. Force is quite the opposite of love. Love gives itself it does not have to be forced.

Suggested Take Away:

- Create a list of self-loving behavior.

- No one is more responsible for me than I am.

- Be to ourselves and others that which we seek. Then what we seek will be.

- Take the time to conduct an assessment of your activities, behavior, and ultimately your choices. See if they line up with the definition of self-love: being kind, patient, gentle, truthful, helpful, nurturing, and supportive. [See the Guide for Example]

FAITH – CHAPTER 3

Faith: the substance of things hoped for [desire] and the evidence of things not seen. A big part of the alignment process is learning to be led by faith. Trusting that what you desire can and will manifest, when you align your thoughts and actions with that which you seek. This process takes awareness, commitment and consistency.

Being led by faith required me tapping into every ounce of courage I could muster up, the process was slow and sometimes painful. I grew to recognize the sensations associated with fear that would rise up in me. I began the habit of using those moments, the moments I felt the sensation of fear rising up in me [MOMENTS OF TRUTH] to pray and meditate.

Ultimately, I responded to the fear with an act of faith. Coming to this place of awareness, developing this new practice was such a life transforming addition to the spiritual journey I was on. It was my next step to experiencing life on purpose. It was a continuous act of me learning to give my ALL to the process of developing a stronger relationship with my spiritual nature.

It was uncomfortable, and it was ambiguous, yet for some reason it was also very beautiful. I was learning how to

The Greatest Gifts of ALL

surrender my will, which had been tainted by the experiences I had and the influence of societal demands, with the will of the Most High. I wanted nothing more than to assist the process as much as I could and so, I had to start looking at life differently.

You see once I opened up to what was happening to and through me, I was no longer just going through the motions of living I was on an assignment. Everything I did, said, and thought took on a more profound meaning. I inner-stood that I/we are a part of something greater bigger than the cars we drive, the type of home we live; bigger than our physical appearances and far bigger than the 'mistakes' we make as we grow through lessons.

Inner-standing this helped increase my faith. I no longer wanted to hold on to things that were no longer or maybe had never served me. I wanted to honor the Divine's will in my life, in this life I'd been chosen to experience and express. I inner-stood on a very real level the more I surrendered to faith the more I mustard up the courage to trust the process by not needing to know how everything was going to line up, the more I gave over my will to the will of the Divine the more my faith increased, life began to make more sense.

The Greatest Gifts of ALL

Faith expanded the possibilities to far beyond anything I could ever imagine in my limited view which at present could only see as far as what I had seen, and what I had seen was clouded by the sensations of fear. However, I now knew that the Most High is unlimited. I now knew that so called miracles were happening every day for people, for me. When my faith was activated I could see these miracles clearly.

I started thinking about how new inventions seemed impossible until someone believe they weren't. I started thinking about how dis-eases were labeled incurable until someone stepped out on faith and kept using their energy to research a cure in spite of popular belief.

When I began to inner-stand that the only limitations in this life that existed are the ones we humans place on this life when we lack the courage and faith to believe, my desire to live by faith increased. I must admit thoughts went through my mind as I stepped out on faith, such as 'What happens if I lose everything.' 'If I don't keep this job or if I don't take just any job so I can pay my bills how will I live, how will I eat, how will I survive?'

Then I would think to myself, would losing everything be so bad if I could exchange them for the experience of peace

(Which holding on to everything I currently had was not giving me anyway). Peace of mind is worth much more than anything I have ever possessed. I now knew, as I've had the experience of the opposite, peace of mind is a priceless blessing and learning the act of faith is key to obtaining this peace.

In terms of surviving in relation to monetary means, there were many days, weeks, months where I lived not knowing how I would pay my bills, or how I would eat, fill my gas tank etc. I realized these were valuable moments on my spiritual journey as well.

I learned to trust the will of God. I learned that my help came from an unlimited infinite source. I begin to see that no matter what God would always provide for me. Whether the Most High sent assistance through my son, Nazyeir, having a grand idea (which he has often), a sister/friend, Semiko, encouraging me by blessing me with a bunch of printed shirts for a business idea, another sister/friend, Kim, sending me money for food when my cupboards were bare, ANOTHER sister/friend requesting that I build her website and financing the process, a kind neighbor who just wanted to share a delicious new recipe they tried, my older sister, Tawana, always being led by God to donate to the cause I working on, my little sister, Nkenge, taking my teen who

The Greatest Gifts of ALL

was challenging me, in for some auntie and nephew bonding time –giving us a much needed break during these challenging financial times, my mom, Sandra, always investing in my latest creation, or my dad, Nathan, being led to give me a car. I really could go on, as, when I walked by faith God just kept showing up! Sometimes it meant I'd ride my bike around town to save gas, which also helped me maintain a healthy body.

The Lesson:

The Divine was teaching me lessons about faith. The Divine was showing me that yes I may have to struggle a little bit on some days (until my mind caught up to the abundance that was all around me), I might not be able to eat as much as I wanted all the time, however; I would eat. I may not have been able to travel as far as I'd like to go every day, however; I would get to where I needed to be to receive the next blessing, and the next lesson. I might have to learn to negotiate with a few debt collectors, however; I was blessed even to have debt (when you think about it).

In essence, the Almighty was showing me that I would always be provided for and further more God was letting me know, that I was meant to do more than just survive. I was meant to thrive and excel in excellence in everything I did.

The Greatest Gifts of ALL

The only way I was going to thrive is if I learned to respond to life in faith. Through these lessons of faith I was learning and receiving what I prayed for in a roundabout way.

I became better equipped to manage my finances, I learned to connect with people better and appreciate all the relationships in my life, and I also in turn built a stronger relationship with myself. Yeah this faith stuff was alright with me. And the more I gave in to it, the more I experienced the Almighty favoring me, showering me with blessings far beyond my wildest dreams. Opening me up even more to the greatest gifts of ALL; however; at first I encountered my fears one by one.

The Message:

Our reactions and responses to life's experiences create our reality. This is such a powerful statement, I'll repeat it again. Our reactions and responses to life's experiences create our reality. On the faith journey I was taught to look at everything from a spiritual perspective. Which to me meant that I was being taken through a series of experiences given to me by the Divine to see how I would handle the experiences, how I would react or respond.

No matter what I experienced or thought of what others I encountered did, I chose not to give too much energy to the

The Greatest Gifts of ALL

external, I shifted my attention and energy instead to how I responded to what they did or what I experienced. This is what mattered most in shaping my character and in me developing spiritually. Be in the world but not of the behavior of the world. In essence, it did not matter what the situation was, what the people around me did, I had to be a vessel for the Divine, I had to be the light in every situation if I wanted to grow and have everything around me grow too. This was my responsibility. I believed, in faith, by me changing the way I responded to people, things, and circumstances my life would change.

We can only control, change, and work on ourselves; leading by example is the true way to teach. When you walk by faith and not by sight, you will again encounter what you previously created in fear; this includes relationships, material challenges, problem solving processes, financial solutions, and health related concerns. These moments of truth are a gift to you, even if they do not feel or appear like a gift at the moment.

During the moments of truth, take a deep breath, set an intention in your mind of the desired outcome. If the moment of truth is a pattern that has repeated itself in your life, you will remember how you responded to the moment in the past. Think of the result that occurred before

The Greatest Gifts of ALL

[Contrast]. Then vividly imagine the desired manifestation. Align your thoughts and actions in the direction of the desired manifestation, no matter how much resistance you feel internally to do so. Remember taking a deep cleansing breath from your belly is your most powerful tool. Proceed, in Faith, knowing the intended outcome can and will manifest in response to your actions.

The Greatest Gifts of ALL

Suggested Take Away

1. Remember on the faith journey you will encounter what you created in fear, again. These are called **Moments of Truth,** giving you the opportunity to respond differently in faith.
2. During moments of truth take a deep cleansing breath from the belly
3. Concentrate your energy on your behavior (your behavior is what will create your reality - the aftermath)
4. Set an intention for the desired outcome
5. Align your thoughts and actions in the direction of the desired manifestation

One with ALL

Deep deep inside
I know I'll find you,
you can't hide
I come from you
you gave me life
to you I must return
I long for you
to see your face
to feel your sweet embrace
my maker
my healer
I give myself to you now
make me whole
complete me
for I am your child
I lay down every burden
every want and desire
at your feet
I surrender my will
you are the first and the last
The alpha and the omega
the beginning and the end
you are
ALL
and so I go deep inside
giving ALL of me
back to ALL of you
In spirit we
are
One

The Greatest Gifts of ALL

MANIFESTATION

EXPERIENCING YOUR DESIRES

The Greatest Gifts of ALL

MY LIFE IS A PRAYER

MY SOULS SPEAKS TO ME
THROUGH THE CHALLENGES I FACE WITH FAITH
EACH DAY THE DIVINE BLESS ME
NEW STRENGTH I FIND
REALIZING I'M BEING PREPARED
MY DESTINY REQUIRES GREATNESS
PATIENCE, COMMITMENT, COURAGE
I'M LEARNING A NEW WAY OF BEING
SEEING, SPEAKING, DREAMING
AND IT FEELS AMAZING
EACH MOMENT UNFOLDS
LIKE A MIRACLE I PRAYED FOR
I AM SO BLESSED
THE DIVINE HAS GIVEN ME ALL
I NEED TO SHINE

SCAN TO LISTEN

facebook.com/investinyouandshine
@investinyouandshine
@investnunshine
www.investinyouandshine.com

The Greatest Gifts of ALL

CONCLUSION

Every day I grew stronger in my awareness, self-love, confidence, and faith. I learned to pay attention to the thoughts, words, and actions I was emanating from my being. I learned to engage in loving practices with myself during moments when I felt all hope was lost, and yearned to feel love; and I learned to have faith in life's process.

I learned to find love within. When I felt like crying I allowed myself to cry without shame, freely and immediately after I would search deep inside to find the strength and direct myself toward a loving practice. These loving practices included deep yogic breathing and dry skin brushing to stimulate the adrenal glands and increase the dopa-mine levels in my body *(visit website for information on these practices www.investinyouandshine.com)*. Singing was another way I learned to love myself through these moments, one of my favorite tunes is, "where the spirit of the Lord is, there is liberty."

I realized these moments were such an important part of me getting stronger in awareness, self-love, faith and belief in myself. These moments where monumental to stepping to the next level of the journey back to higher self. The Divine wanted me to dig deep within.

The Greatest Gifts of ALL

It is on soul purpose that we experience moments of loneliness, it is on purpose that we experience moments where we are not able to call on a friend. You know the moments I'm speaking of, when all you want to do is reach out, yet for some odd reason it seems no one is around. These are the moments the Divine is asking us to reach in and find that inner strength: the self-love, the peace that passes all understanding.

This strength is necessary, not so that we can get used to being alone with our lessons, not so that we become solely independent, however; it is so that we can become whole. As we become whole we are able to be of more service in our purpose. We are able to be more nurturing in our homes. We become better equipped to walk by faith and not by sight, allowing the Divine will to manifest in our lives. We've been given the simplest tools to accomplish Divine manifestation in our lives: awareness, self-love, and faith, "The Greatest Gifts of ALL."

The Greatest Gifts of ALL

Definitions:

ALIGNMENT: getting yourself into position: reprogramming your thoughts and changing your actions

ALL – Source Energy, essence of which we beings & spiritual energies derive - the Divine

CHAKRAS: [Sanskrit translation: wheel or disk] Wheels of energy within and around the body. There are 7 main chakras aligning the spine. These chakras start from the base of the spine through to the crown of the head. The wheels of energy correspond to nerve centers within the body. Ideally the wheels of energy known as the chakras must remain opened, aligned and flowing fluidly.

CONTRASTS: Patterns, Energy, circumstances, and relationships you no longer/or never wanted to purposefully experience in life. **SUCH AS:** Fear, frustration, & Anger

DESIRE: THE DREAMS IN YOUR SOUL YOU'RE BORN TO EXPERIENCE

DIVINE: Collective Consciousness

E.G.O.: External Guidance Overload

INNER-STAND: Spiritually connecting with an experience in a way that allows the Divine to use the experience as a teachable lesson helping us to see the purpose of the experience.

INTENTIONS: What you desire to happen as a result of your thoughts and actions

The Greatest Gifts of ALL

I.G.D.: Internal guided direction

MEDITATION: Medicine for the mind. Engaging in moments of stillness. Bringing attention to the expansion and retraction of your breath while focusing on a centering thought, visualization, or breath; for the purpose of experiencing mind, body soul wellness by: balancing the hormones, aligning the chakras, calming of the mind, expulsion of toxins, and increase in the flow of oxygen in the body.

MOMENTS OF TRUTH: Internally identifiable moments when you are aware that you feel afraid/stuck/confused/alone/anxious/depressed. During these moments, sensations are staring you in the face, rising up in your belly, penetrating your thoughts and you are a witness to experiencing the contrast of what you desire.

It is this moment that you are challenged to react based on previous experiences or be present in the moment and respond in a way that will propel you forward into a new direction so that you can allow the universe to help you grow closer to your purpose. The question at hand is: Will you fall back into your old comfortable ways of being, or will you rise to the next level embracing the ability for life to show you something new and true to your destiny? (***Tip during these moments, go slow***)

SAMSKARAS – Habitual patterns

SELF-LOVE: being kind, patient, gentle, truthful, helpful, nurturing, and supportive to one's self and others [others we encounter are simply an extension of ourselves].

The Greatest Gifts of ALL

YOGA: A physical, mental, and spiritual practice consisting of asanas [physical postures] and ways of thinking, speaking, and being in alignment with creating physical, mental AND SPIRITUAL HARMONY.

After Note:

I decided to begin focusing on the beauty that makes up life and learn to see the experiences as lessons directing me toward my soul purpose.

One of my favorite quotes comes from Maya Angelou, "The most challenging thing about being the teacher is living the lessons first." I lived through the lessons and so I can not only relate and empathize with others who have or are going through feelings of anxiety, depression, and insecurity. I now know why these feelings come and how to rise above. There is always a purpose.

Finding my way through the lessons caused me to connect with yoga, meditation, and my creative gifts; allowing me to achieve mind, body, and soul wellness. This connection transformed my life and now I am living out my greatest dreams and deepest desires.

I realized the challenges, and ultimately the experience those challenges bring, were the greatest gifts of ALL.

May blessing of abundant peace, health, and wealth be with you always.

~ **Ashe**

The Greatest Gifts of ALL

Contact Information

S.H.I.N.E. INC.

MAIN WEBSITE: www.investinyouandshine.com

EMAIL: investinyouandshine@gmail.com

The Greatest Gifts of ALL

Stay Tuned
4
The Next Creative
Expression:

"Letters to My Sister"

Focus Your Mind

ABOUT THE AUTHOR

In 2013 I realized that I had developed a habit of not listening to my heart which was killing me softly robbing me of the opportunity to experience the magnificence of creation. My soul was crying out to me; and on a cold day in March of 2013 I answered that cry. I stepped out on faith and started saying yes to my purpose. Everything I dreamed of doing 'WHEN I HAD TIME, COURAGE, ABILTIY' I began making time for, developing courage for, and learning more about; because I inner-stood these things were important to my soul and ultimately my purpose. My question to you is: **what are YOU saying YES to in your life?** Let's build on this. Reach me at: www.investinyouandshine.com

The Greatest Gifts of ALL

Who I've Created:

- Founder of S.H.I.N.E. Inc.
- Registered Yoga Instructor – RYT 200 (Yoga Alliance Member)
- **Author: "The Greatest Gifts of ALL"**
- Mind, Body, & Soul Wellness Guide

Education & Credentials:

- Bachelor Degree in the Science of Management 2012
- Child Development Associate Certification 2013
- 200 – Hour Teacher Training Course at A Jewel in the Lotus 2014
- Doctor of Naturopathic Medicine (ND) Exp. January 2020
- CPR/AED Certification – On going

Alignment Process Guide

Instructions

- The process of manifesting our desires comes in 4 stages.
- These stages present themselves repeatedly at different levels of the process.
- The stages consist of the following:
  Contrast (The thing you are working to change presents itself)
  Desire (You begin to want to experience something else instead)
  Alignment (You position yourself to experience the thing you desire)
  Manifestation (You receive the thing you desire)
- Set your intention to align yourself with the steps necessary to achieve the desired manifestation and work on completely aligning yourself.
- During the process when you are faced with a challenge, this means it is time to level up. Time to study more, time to go deeper in your practices.
- Look at the areas on this list that could use improving and work toward developing the area more.
- If an area really challenges you create a themed vision board related to the development of that area.

The Greatest Gifts of ALL

Practical Alignment Focused Techniques to Implement

- *Improve your water intake:*

  This is an important component for helping your body to maintain balance. A balanced body will allow energy to flow well through your chakras keeping your body fully aligned

  Drink half your body weight in ounces of water (There are 8 ounces in a cup)

  Set a reminder in your phone to for specific times of day to drink water

- *Practice deep breathing from the belly often (inhale to the count of 4 hold to the count of 2 exhale to the count of 4)*

  Breathing deep helps oxygen to penetrate the cells and allows the nutrients to flow to the appropriate organs.

  Helps to calm the nervous system, and propels lymph fluids along the lymphatic system (*important for immune strength)

  Begin a regular meditation practice

  Set a reminder in your phone to remind you to breath deep

The Greatest Gifts of ALL

- *Keep an affirmation journal*

  *You want to reprogram your brain to a new way
  of thinking and train it to focus on one intention
  at a time to improve concentration*

  *Develop an affirmation specific to your current
  desire and work to write that affirmation across
  5 sheets of your journal notebook daily (One
  sentence of the affirmation on each line)*

  *When you begin to feel your energy at a high
  level (which means it is trying to uncoil, and
  having a difficult time processing) use this time
  to sit and do your affirmation journal, to
  reprogram your thoughts around your intention*

- *Decalcify the pineal gland*

  **STEP 1 – Remove these to stop further calcification
  of your Pineal Gland**

  1. Halides (Fluoride, Chlorine and Bromide)

  2. Tap Water

  3. Pesticides

  4. Sugar, Caffeine, Alcohol and Tobacco (S.C.A.T.)

STEP 2 – Remove existing calcification within your
   Pineal Gland using the following:

1. Organic Blue Ice Skate Fish Oil

2. MSM (organic sulfur compound)

3. Raw Chocolate

4. Citric Acid

5. Garlic

6. Raw Apple Cider Vinegar

7. Oregano oil and Neem extract

8. Vitamin K1/K2

9. Boron

10. Melatonin

11. Iodine

12. Tamarind

13. Distilled Water

14. Nigella Sativa (the black seed)

15. Zeolite

16. Chaga Mushroom

17. Yoga

- *Keep chakra alignment music playing at all times*

     Many of the habits that caused you to experience the contrast (things you do not want to continue to experience) are embedded deep in your subconscious.

     Playing soft chakra aligning music while you work, sleep, and be will assist with the alignment process on levels you may not be familiar with connecting to

     You can find some sources on YouTube (check out some of the ones we like on our YouTube channel.) You can find our channel by visiting the website at: www.investinyouandshine.com

- *Create a vision board*

     See our Effective Vision Board E-Book Guide for more details on constructing an effective vision board (www.investinyouandshine.com – Services - Vision Board)

The Greatest Gifts of ALL

- *Follow the following steps when you are challenged by the waiting stages of the alignment process (it is important to prepare and position yourself to receive the intention, this is the act of faith, showing the universe you believe it will happen).*

  o *Pray*
  o *Meditate*
  o *Share your concern about the process someone you trust*
  o *Create something (this will help focus your mind on something productive)*
  o *Try a new recipe*
  o *Take a class*
  o *Organize*
  o *Clean*
  o *Rest*

Believe in Yourself

SPOKEN WORD

SCAN THE BARCODE SO YOU CAN LISTEN TO THE POEM

Writing is a cathartic way to release, emotionally, what is no longer serving us, turning ashes into a beautiful artistic, linguistic display of spoken word.

The Greatest Gifts of ALL

I STAND IN REVERENCE OF THE DIVINE

I COVET HEALING
OVER THE THINGS THAT CHALLENGE
AND THE STRENGTH TO RISE ABOVE
DEEPLY I BREATH
SEEKING POWER FROM THE SOURCE
OF ALL I AM
THIS EXPERIENCE IS SACRED
EACH MOMENT DESIGNED
WITH PURPOSE
I EMBRACE THE LESSONS SO I MAY GROW
I AM THAT, I AM
A SHINING BEING DWELLING IN LIGHT
MANIFESTED AND CREATED BY THE LIMBS
OF THE ALMIGHTY DIVINE CREATOR
EVERYTHING I NEED IS WITHIN ME
I DIG DEEP TO FIND PEACE
MY FAITH IS RESTORED
UNSHAKEN
COMMITTED
TRUSTING THE DIVINE
WE ARE ONE
THE HIGHER I GO
THE STRONGER I GROW
NEW REVELATIONS DAILY
THERE IS POWER AND GREATNESS IN SILENCE
I EMBRACE IT
I AM GRANTED THE KEYS
DOORS UNLOCK WITH THE TOUCH OF MY HAND
I STAND IN REVERENCE OF THE DIVINE

facebook.com/investinyouandshine
@investinyouandshine
@investnunshine
www.investinyouandshine.com

SCAN TO LISTEN

The Greatest Gifts of ALL

The True Way

Unconsciously people do what was done to them
To themselves and everyone around
The vibrational energy creates more than a sound
A pattern is set in motion
A system, a habit, generational way
To see it one has to be still
To change it one must grow within
Dig deep to find the true way
A challenge indeed
To master the seed
Which germinates before it is seen
At first no light
Darkness produces
Desire to align and be free
It happened to he, it happened to she,
It even happened to me
So i rolled up my sleeves
And paid close attention
To what life had to say
The guides were there
The lessons were clear
I became a student of the Divine
I was taught that self-love
Awareness and reflection
Was ALL I needed to SHINE

SCAN TO LISTEN

facebook.com/investinyouandshine
@investinyouandshine
@investnunshine
www.investinyouandshine.com

The Greatest Gifts of ALL

Handing Him Over Your Heart

Does he know his worth
If not he'll never know yours
His concentration
Will be how you can
Benefit, entertain and
stimulate him
Fancy his whims
Nurture his belly
Carry his seed
Impress his friends
With how he fills his needs
Is he interested in you?
Compliment what you do?
Take the time to adore you?
How he treats his momma
Does he give her much drama
Then maybe he needs to be alone
Spend some time with God
Get in touch with mother nature
Until he bows down to that which he came
Cherishes the womb which held his life
You'd want to be careful
With handing him over your heart

The Greatest Gifts of ALL

EXPANDING MY REACH

Cold came, wind changed
And it seemed like everything was gone
Like i was standing on a line too damn long
All I kept hearing was be strong
Ancestors whispering troubles don't last long
Like a storm casting a shadow in the sky
As it hurries by
My days were dark and my nights were lonely
Praying for God to hold me
I learned how to activate faith
I learned how to wait and meditate
Change is like a revolution for the soul
It creeps up on you like a hunger pain
Borderline insane
Gotta keep looking up
Keep digging deep
Tossing and turning in my sleep
Like what is peace?
Is it meant for me?
Keeping my eyes on the Journey
Cause I know there is a way
And a lot of it has to do with what i say
I co-creator manifesting my beliefs
so I'm monitoring what I speak
Practicing what I preach
Expanding my reach…

SCAN TO LISTEN

facebook.com/investinyouandshine
@investinyouandshine
@investnunshine
www.investinyouandshine.com

The Greatest Gifts of ALL

MY LIFE IS A PRAYER

MY SOULS SPEAKS TO ME
THROUGH THE CHALLENGES I FACE WITH FAITH
EACH DAY THE DIVINE BLESS ME
NEW STRENGTH I FIND
REALIZING I'M BEING PREPARED
MY DESTINY REQUIRES GREATNESS
PATIENCE, COMMITMENT, COURAGE
I'M LEARNING A NEW WAY OF BEING
SEEING, SPEAKING, DREAMING
AND IT FEELS AMAZING
EACH MOMENT UNFOLDS
LIKE A MIRACLE I PRAYED FOR
I AM SO BLESSED
THE DIVINE HAS GIVEN ME ALL
I NEED TO SHINE

SCAN TO LISTEN

facebook.com/investinyouandshine
@investinyouandshine
@investnunshine
www.investinyouandshine.com

The Greatest Gifts of ALL

ALL

I WAS WHO LIFE CREATED
NOW I RE-CREATE MYSELF
TAKING GOD'S TIME
TO STRENGTHEN MY MIND
EMBRACING ALL THE WEALTH
LEARNING SELF-LOVE
FORGIVENESS TRUST FAITH
BEING ON PURPOSE. SPEAKING ON PURPOSE.
THE ALMIGHTY DIVINE CREATOR
IS PURIFYING MY SOUL
SHE, AND HE, AND THEY AWAKE ME
AND NOW THE LIGHTS SO BRIGHT
IN AWE OF GOD'S CREATENESS
I STAY CLOSE TO MY GUIDES
I YEARN TO INNER STAND
I WILL WHEN IT'S TIME
- APRIL DIANE

Visit the website to read more
& purchase your copy today.
www.investinyouandshine.com

The Greatest Gifts of ALL

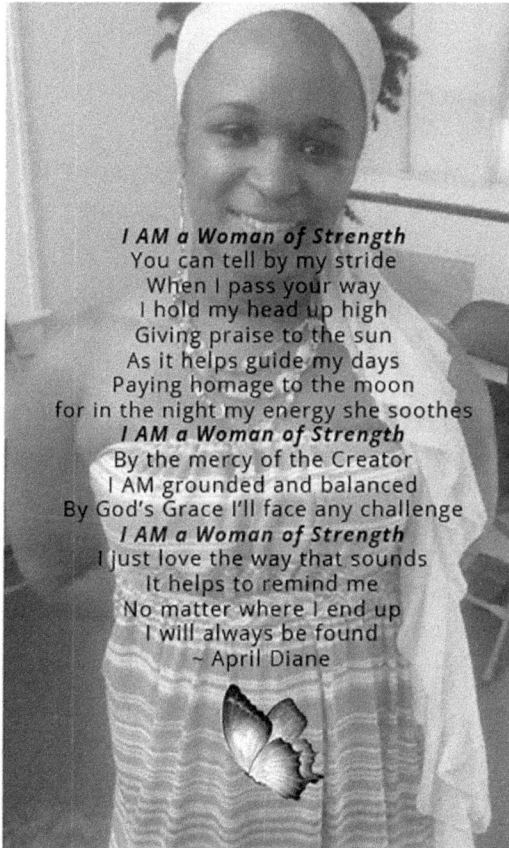

I AM a Woman of Strength
You can tell by my stride
When I pass your way
I hold my head up high
Giving praise to the sun
As it helps guide my days
Paying homage to the moon
for in the night my energy she soothes
I AM a Woman of Strength
By the mercy of the Creator
I AM grounded and balanced
By God's Grace I'll face any challenge
I AM a Woman of Strength
I just love the way that sounds
It helps to remind me
No matter where I end up
I will always be found
~ April Diane

The Greatest Gifts of ALL

Thank You For listening

~ Be Well

The Greatest Gifts of ALL

www.ingramcontent.com/pod-product-compliance
Lightning Source LLC
Chambersburg PA
CBHW071417040426
42445CB00012BA/1189